KLIPWORKS

A guide to strategic mobile
video production

KLIPWORKS

Edition 1, 2018. klipworks.com

CONTENT

Preface	1
Chapter 1: Project Scoping	3
Chapter 2: Conceptualization	9
Chapter 3: Deciding On An Idea	18
Chapter 4: Planning A Pilot Test	22
Chapter 5: Preparation	29
Chapter 6: Recording	43
Chapter 7: Editing	51
Summary	55

KLIPWORKS

PREFACE

*"The best camera
is the one that's with you"*

There are countless stories out there for you to tell, and with your smartphone always at hand you have the opportunity to press record in seconds no matter where you are. With the power of video your stories can come to life and help you get your message across quicker and more engaging than ever.

Yet creating videos that are clear and concise in their imagery and messaging can be difficult. This is why we created this ebook - to empower content creators to make engaging videos and use them strategically.

We believe that with the right knowledge anyone can become an outstanding video content creator, and we are here to help you achieve that.

*Sincerely,
Klipworks*

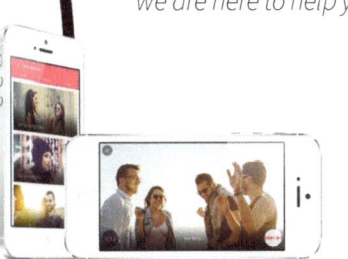

CHAPTER 1

PROJECT SCOPING

"Clarity of vision is the key to achieving your objectives"

Before you jump into recording your video you should set aside a bit of time to outline the scope of your video project, and consider what strategic role you want video to play in your specific context.

In short you want to set a clear purpose for the content you are about to create.

WORKING IN COMMUNICATIONS/HR/PR YOU MIGHT WANT TO ACHIEVE

1. More efficient communication with internal and external stakeholders
2. Better recruitment
3. Education of a particular customer segment
4. Increased following on social media

WORKING IN MARKETING/SALES/CUSTOMER SUCCESS YOU MIGHT WANT TO ACHIEVE

1. Increased brand awareness in the digital ecosystem
2. Higher engagement from a specific customer segment
3. More qualified leads for sales
4. More engaging content for specific stages of their customer journey

Your guiding beacon should always be the potential benefit of your video to the intended viewer.

Get into this mindset and you will have a much easier time figuring out what purpose your videos should serve. If you get this right you are on the path to soaring engagement rates.

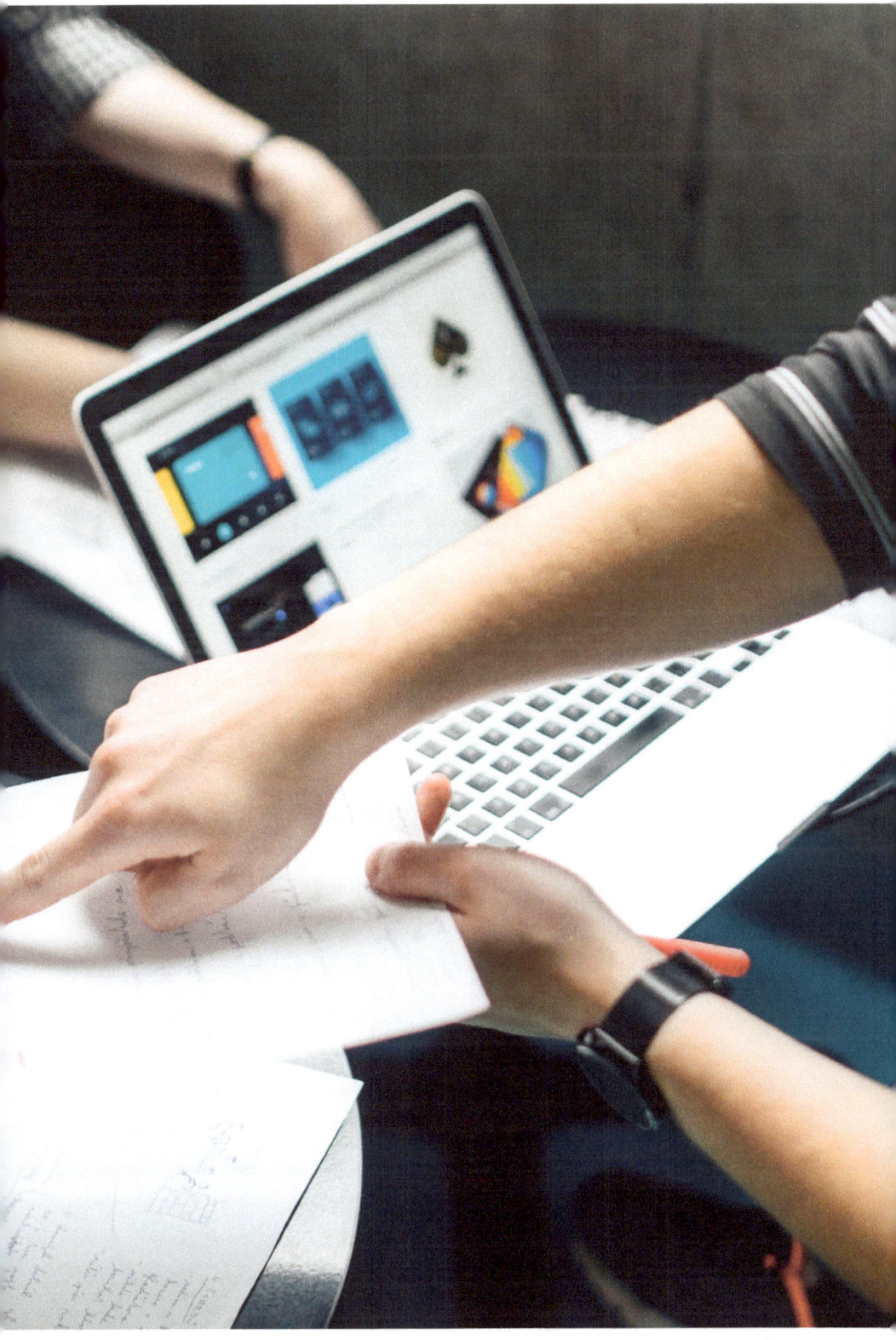

FORMULATE A VIDEO MISSION STATEMENT

To stay focused and have your team and external collaborators stay on the same track we advocate formulating a simple video mission statement.

Here is an example of what it could look like with placeholders for you to fill in:

At [Company name], we make [adjective] video content for [your target audience] on [your platforms of choice], to have them [define your desired outcome].

Pro tip: Don't bite off more than you can chew

People often get overly ambitious with their video projects, and end up getting discouraged when faced with the challenges that often surface in a production. Keep it simple at first, focus on making smaller video projects and let your creativity and ambitions grow from there.

CHAPTER 2

CONCEPTUALIZATION

"The difficulty lies not in developing new ideas,
but in escaping from old ones"

You might already have an idea about what kind of videos you want to create but maybe you are in need of a bit of inspiration to hone in on a good concept.

Either way we suggest putting your brain-cells to work on conceptualizing your video project to lay down the creative bedrock.

GET SOME INSPIRATION

Coming up with a concept from scratch can be tough which is why it makes sense for you to get some inspiration from the video content already out there.

There are massive amounts of video on the web for you to get inspired by and we suggest browsing the most common video platforms taking note of interesting, funny and inspirational videos you encounter along the way.

BROWSE YOUTUBE, FACEBOOK, INSTAGRAM AND LINKEDIN

1. Search for videos in your niche and take note of what people are doing well.

2. See if you can find channels dedicated to making videos that relate to your field of work and browse through the content of influencers in your space.

3. Check out your competitors and learn from their success and mistakes.

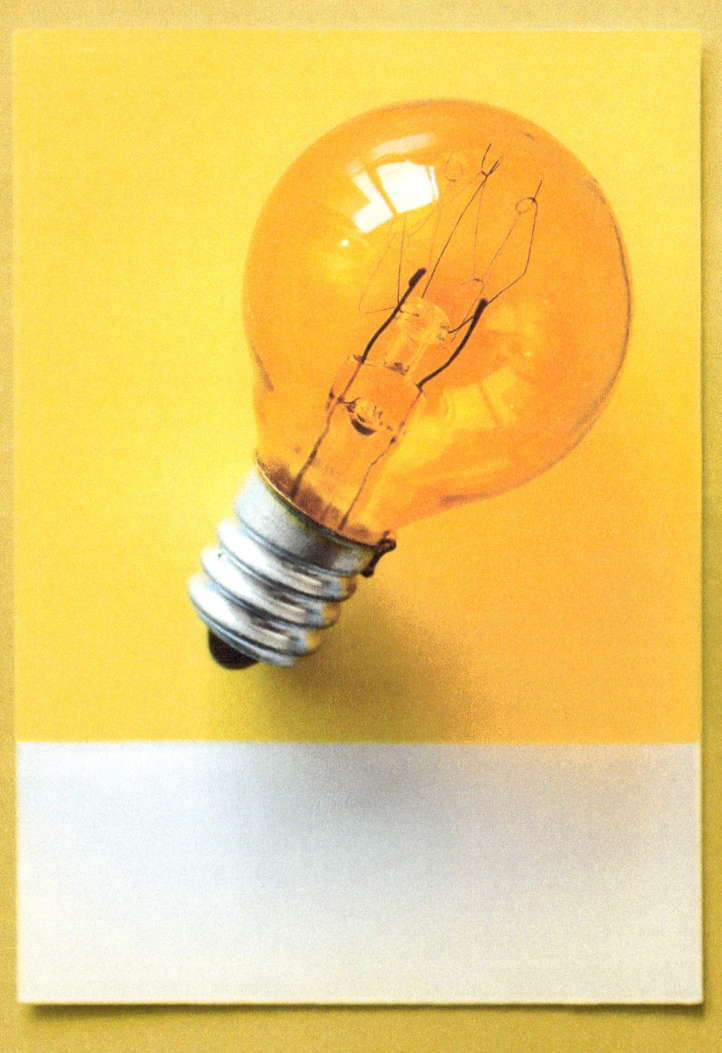

FAMILIARIZE YOURSELF WITH DIFFERENT VIDEO TYPES

Looking through a bunch of videos you will quickly notice that there are differences between the type of videos people create. From an overall perspective you can pigeonhole videos into three categories.

REPORTAGE

This style of video is characterized by having someone report on a specific event or interview a specific subject. The main focus is to document the event or convey the sentiments of the interviewee.

VLOGS

Vlogs are videos that are very minimalistic often only comprising 1 person, 1 camera and maybe even 1-take. These types of videos are very personality driven and often more opinionated than you see in reportage style videos.

TEXT & VOICEOVER BASED

These types of videos are characterised by being less personal in their expression. They often do not contain an identifiable reporter or moderator, and rely on text or voiceovers to convey their message.

Ask yourself what type of category would be a good space for you to work in and how it could support your video mission statement. Let these assumptions guide you in the next step of the process; brainstorming for ideas.

BRAINSTORM FOR CONCEPTS

Having followed the preceeding steps your head should now be full of inspiration and ready for a fruitful brainstorming session.

Brainstorming with your team or by yourself is a excellent way to get the creative juices flowing. Keep your video mission statement in mind and follow the basic principles of productive brainstorming:

1. Start by brainstorming alone for a few minutes, so you don't get affected by the ideas of others
2. Prioritize quantity of ideas over quality, you want everything on the table to start with
3. Remember that playfulness is key to creativity
4. Don't judge and analyze the ideas at the outset
5. Encourage crazy and quirky ideas
6. Let everyone have a say

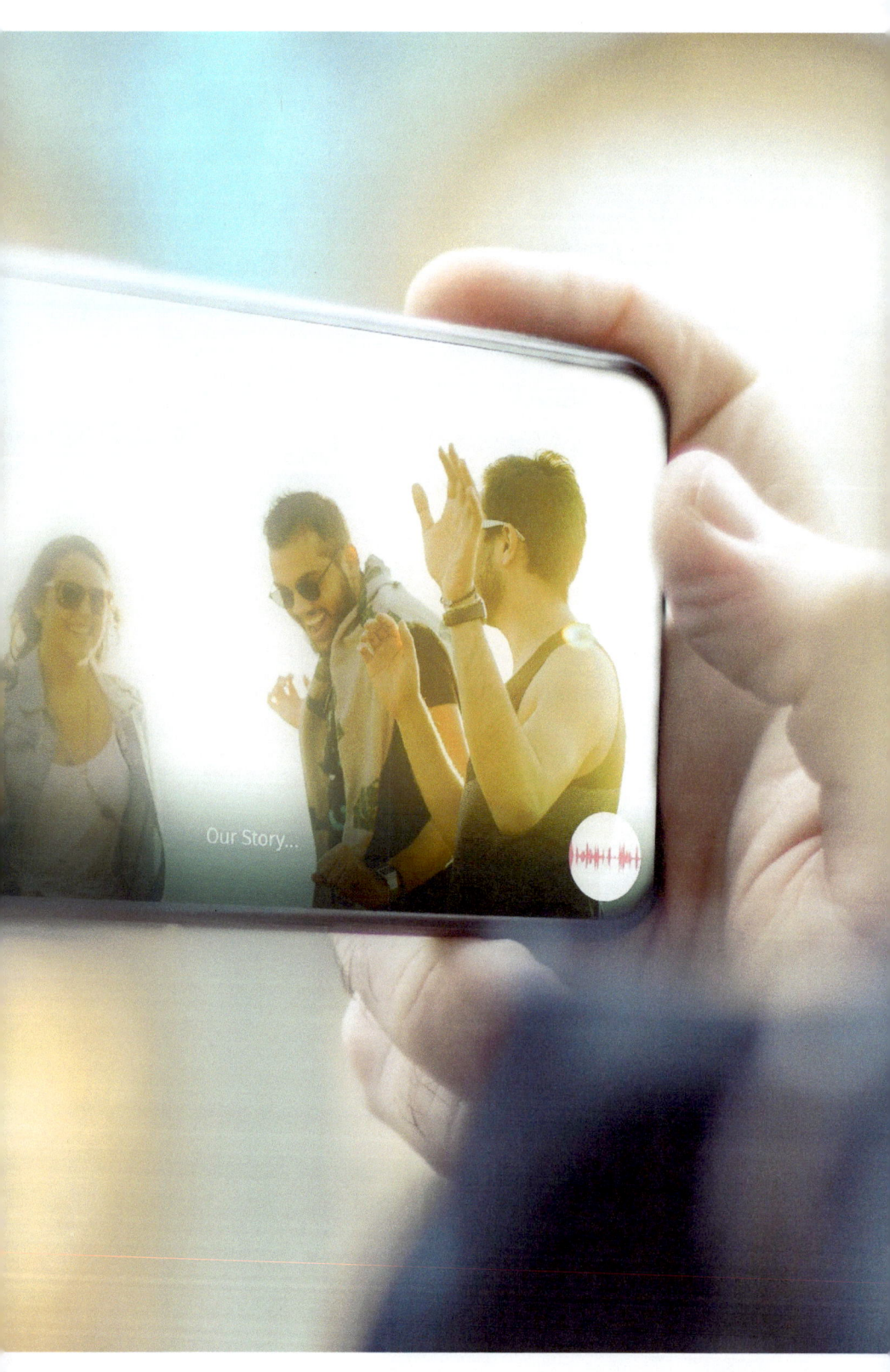

Document all ideas by mapping them out on paper or visually on a whiteboard and feel free to express them using words, images etc.

DISTILL YOUR IDEAS

As your brainstorming session progresses you will be able to weed out the bad ideas and see good ones emerging. After a little while you can start refining the ideas that have potential.

THE BEST OF YOUR IDEAS SHOULD ENCOMPASS THE FOLLOWING

1. Relevance - They have to be relevant to your video mission statement.
2. Value providing - They should be able to provide value to your intended audience.
3. Viability - They have to be viable within the limits of your resources.
4. Uniqueness - They should have room for you to add some unique flavour to them.

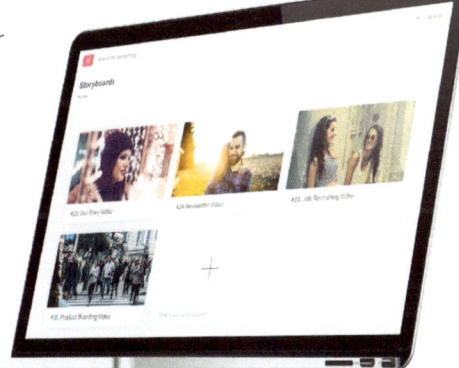

5. Acceptable cost-benefit - They should be able to give you more value in return for your time, energy and money invested in making them.

Pro tip: Choose no more than 3 ideas

Try boiling your ideas down to 3 possible projects. This forces you to make decisions on what to cut out and what has potential, and will ease the final decision making.

CHAPTER 3

DECIDING ON AN IDEA

"The hardest decisions in life are not between
good and bad or right and wrong,
but between two goods or two rights."

At this point in your ideation phase you should have 3 solid concepts to choose from. In most cases you will want to choose only one of them and then go on to test the concept.

The question is how do you choose which one to pursue? You will probably have to consider other factors than just the quality of the ideas themselves as they can be equally good.

CONSIDER THESE FACTORS, WHEN CHOOSING AN IDEA

TIME-SCOPE OF EXECUTION

Ask yourself how long your concept will take to come to life. You might find that some ideas naturally have a longer execution time, which could be a hindrance to realizing the project.

RELEVANCE TO CURRENT CONTEXT/SITUATION

Ask yourself if some of your ideas are more relevant to your current situation or dependent on particular circumstances. If you have a number of events coming up with interesting keynote speakers an interview series with influencers in your industry might be very relevant.

PERSONAL/TEAM MOTIVATION

Your own motivation to follow through on the project is not to be underestimated. The personal drive of you and your team members will have a big impact on the quality of your project and motivation can be a deciding factor in whether you succeed or not.

CONTENT LONGEVITY

This factor ties into the cost/benefit analysis of your project. The end results of some ideas will have greater longevity than others based on the value they convey to your audience.

Once you have assessed you ideas in regards to the factors above you should have an idea that comes out as a winner - an idea that can be executed in the foreseeable future, is relevant to your current situation, would be exciting to make and will provide value to your audience for some time to come.

CHAPTER 4

PLANNING A PILOT TEST

"Testing leads to failure,
and failure leads to understanding"

Any good video project takes planning and preparation to become a success and even though you might feel all set to jump into the deep end you should consider pilot testing your idea. This will give you an opportunity to work out the kinks in your production before show time.

A pilot is basically a small scale test of your production. This approach to testing can be seen in everything from TV production to the world of academia and no matter where you see it the main principle is the same; mock up so you don't mess up.

TRAITS OF A PILOT TEST

So what are the main traits of a pilot test? Good question let's take a look:

1. It's an execution of your project at a small scale
2. It utilizes simulation and/or mock-up situations e.g. fake interviews and staged events
3. It's tested on a sample audience for feedback

The real strength in doing pilot testing of any kind lies in the fact that it gives you room to fail without consequences. If you mess up your pilot there will only be insignificant repercussions, and you will have learned a lot that can be applied to future video projects.

TYPICAL LEARNINGS FROM PILOT TESTING

Pilot testing will give you a lot of learnings on a number of aspects of your video project.

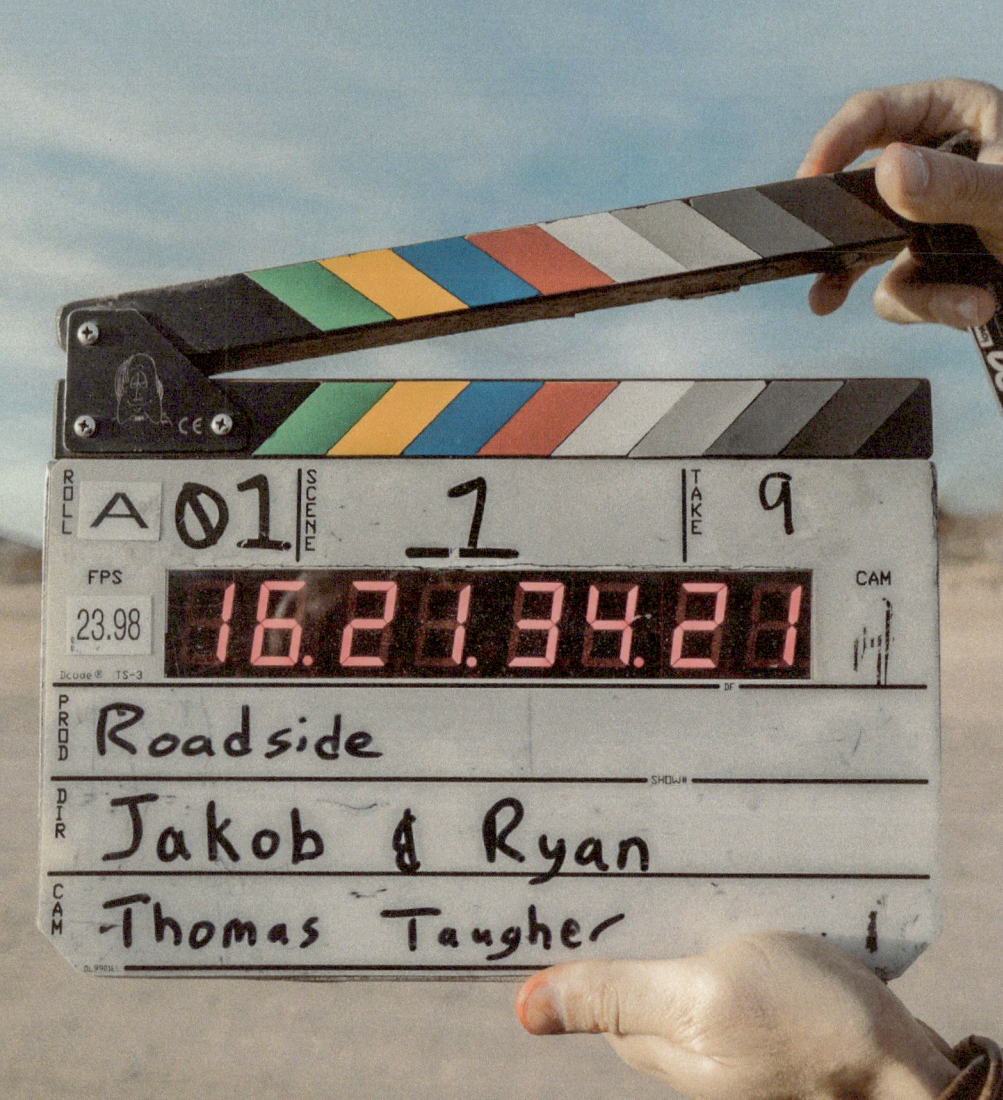

FEASIBILITY

For starters, pilot testing your project will give you a general idea of how doable your project is. Often small things can prove to be a challenge, and if your idea is already giving you a lot of problems in the test phase you might want to iterate it.

TIME

Estimating the amount of time it takes to realize a project can be very tricky. The test phase will give your a good idea of how long the different parts of your pre- and post-production will take.

COST

Running a preliminary test will make the budgeting for your video project somewhat easier. You might uncover some hidden costs that have to be considered in you project.

GEAR

This is an important one, even professionals make mistakes in their set up and you don't want to have problems with your video rig on the day of your shoot. Your pilot test will give you plenty of opportunity to test the settings on your smartphone, the lighting, post-production etc. so you don't get caught unprepared when it counts.

SET UP

The quality of your video can often be traced back to how you set up your shot and even simple situations such as interviews or b-roll takes can prove to be more tricky than anticipated. Without the stress of having to get it 100% right in your pilot, you have the time to test different set ups and learn from any mistakes you make.

QUESTIONING

This one boils down to the intricacies of preparing questions for interviews. One thing is to have it all planned out on paper, another is actually conducting the interview and interacting with the interviewee. Running a mock interview will quickly give you an idea of the quality of your questions, and any need for iteration there might be.

IDEA QUALITY

Put simply, your test project will undoubtedly expose if your idea actually works in reality. At times ideas that seem funny, inspirational or educational on paper fall flat in reality.

Running a pilot test of your video is a must with any new project you are planning to embark on. Even a very small scale testrun will give you valuable insights you can use in your video project, and provide you with a proof of concept to assess before jumping into the real deal.

CHAPTER 5

PREPARATION

"The preparation is what allows success to happen naturally"

Preparation is key to making a good video and in your planning phase you should ask yourself a number of questions:

1. Who do I want to film?
2. What should i say?
3. Where do I want to film?
4. What recordings do I need?

When answered, these questions will result in a clear outline of your cast, script locations and shotlist.

CAST AND INTERVIEWS

The cast of your video depends on the type of video you have decided to make. Maybe you are looking to do an interview, a vlog of yourself or an event video filming a number of participants.

In any case you will have to put some thought into what to ask, say and how you want to present people in your video.

Let us briefly address the fundamentals of a good interview and how to talk to your audience when on camera.

THE CRAFT OF INTERVIEWING

Doing interviews is a craft and takes time and experience to master. But knowing the basics will get you far in conducting your own interviews.

The main principle to have in mind is that your responsibility as the interviewer is to ask good questions that draw out the arguments, experiences and knowledge of the interviewee.

You can start by asking yourself: What is the main goal of this interview and how can my questions help us arrive at that specific goal?

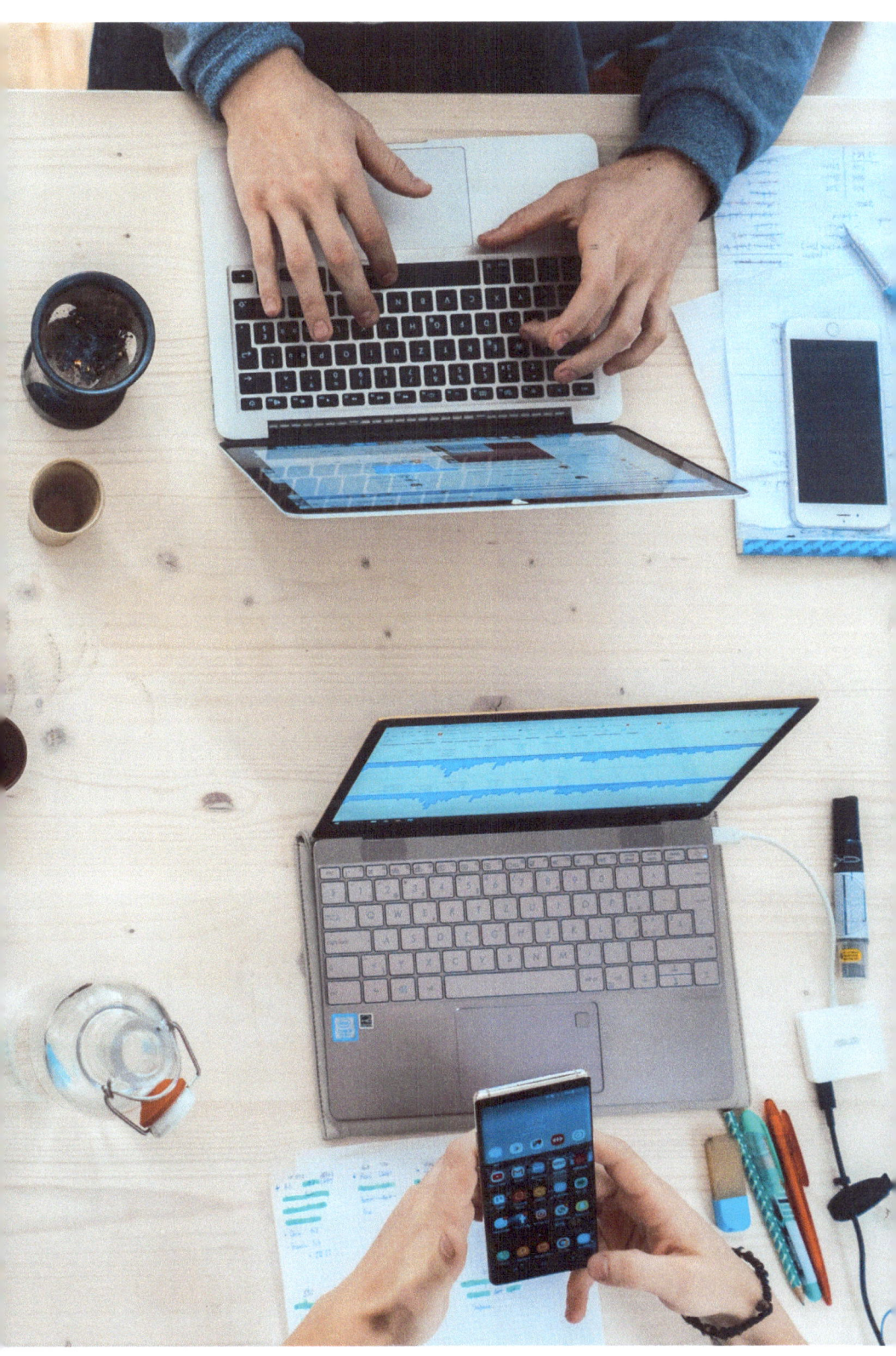

Remember that an interview is not a conversation, but rather a method for you to draw out the thoughts of the interviewee on a specific topic.

You, as an interviewer have a responsibility to achieve this through good questioning and a sensible responsiveness to the answers of the interviewee.

GOOD QUESTIONS

HOW TO ASK THE RIGHT QUESTIONS

Asking good questions is at the core of conducting a good interview.

To arrive at the good questions you can start by asking yourself what is the main story that needs to be told in this interview and how do I draw that story out through my questions.

LET'S LOOK AT AN EXAMPLE

Your package delivery company has just released a new app that makes it a lot easier for your customers to track and receive their packages, and you are interviewing the Head of Product on the features of the app.

What is the story here? Well the most interesting story here is of course the benefits of the app to the end consumer - the fact that they can feel less anxious waiting for their delivery and have more control of when and where to recieve their packages.

GOOD QUESTIONS IN THIS INTERVIEW COULD BE

1. What can your consumers expect from the new app?
2. How does the new app help people monitor their deliveries?
3. Why should the consumer start using the new app?

Pro tip: Always ask open-ended-questions

Open-ended-questions are questions that start with a why, what, how, where etc. and require full sentence answers. These types of questions will provide you with more interesting answers than a simple yes or no.

SCRIPT

When jumping into your very first appearance on camera it can be difficult getting your head around what to actually say.

How do you prepare for when the lights are on and the camera is recording? To help you we have put together some simple tips that you can refer to before the record-button is pressed. As a rule of thumb remember to keep it simple.

ADDRESS THE VIEWER WITH THE PRONOUN "YOU" AS SOON AS POSSIBLE

Studies show that the sooner you can use the word "you" in your video, the more appealing it will be to your viewer. By focusing on the viewer within the first 5-10 seconds of your video you are more likely to get and keep their attention.

CONVEY NO MORE THAN THREE MESSAGES

Don't add more than three messages in the same video, preferably only one if you can. If you need to add more than three messages you should consider splitting the video into two or more videos.

The clearer your focus is the higher the chance of your viewer actually remembering your point.

REPEAT YOUR CALL-TO-ACTION THROUGHOUT THE VIDEO

Include a call to action. It is crucial to consider what the purpose of the video is. What do you want the viewer to do after seeing your video? Don't be afraid to say it many times during the video and in a direct way.

Be very clear on what the viewer should take away from this video and underline it again in the last 10 seconds of your video.

DON'T CLING TO YOUR SCRIPT

Write the script : and throw it away.

The key to a good video is that the viewer doesn't get the feeling that you are reading from a piece of paper.

If you prepared well, it should be fairly easy to remember the main points that you want to get across to the viewer. If you don't nail it exactly as planned, the viewers don't know you messed up since they have no idea what the original script was.

Not relying on a piece of paper will force you to be totally present during the recording : and the luxury is that you can always do the recording again and again until you feel you've got it right.

And if you do the same take five times chances are that you can probably come a long way with a little bit of editing between the different takes.

LOCATIONS

Choosing the right locations to film can have a significant impact on the quality of your video.

LIGHT CONDITIONS

A lot of people underestimate the amount of light required on set. Especially indoors poor light conditions can quickly ruin your shot. Make sure your location is sufficiently illuminated either by natural light or artificial lighting.

SOUND CONDITIONS

If you are recording an interview or a video where you are speaking it is paramount that you assess the level of background noise. Sound is one of the most difficult elements to edit in post production, which is why you want to get it right when recording. Preferably use an external microphone and find a quiet place to record.

LOCATION RELEVANCE

Consider if there are locations that support the subject or message of the video. At times a location can contribute a lot to the story being told in the video. Contemplate for a moment the difference between a journalist reporting directly from parliament versus from a studio on a story about the enactment of a new law - quite a profound difference right?

CREATING A SHOTLIST

Before recording it's a good idea to have an outline of the different shots you need to make up your video. This type of overview is typically referred to as your shotlist.

What your shotlist looks like is of course dependent on the kind of video you are shooting, but there are some basic principles that are applicable to most types of videos that will help you get the shots you need to make a great video.

A- AND B-ROLL FOOTAGE

From an overall perspective you can divide the shots you need into two categories, namely A- and B-roll footage.

A-roll footage is basically the core footage you need for telling your story. It could be the main parts of your interview or your main monologue.

B-roll footage is supplemental footage that provides additional visuals to support what is being told in your main story. An example of the use of B-roll footage could be to cut to recordings of what is being mentioned in you interview while letting the audiotrack from the A-roll footage continue.

Let's say that the interviewee is talking about a new product and you show footage of the product for a few seconds. That's a typical use of B-roll footage.

The reason you want to combine these two types of recordings is because it will make your video much more exciting to watch. Without it you will experience that your videos can come off as monotonous due to the lack of visual variance.

Pro tip: Keep your B-roll shots to at least 10 seconds

People tend to underestimate how long their B-roll footage should be. A good rule of thumb is that each B-roll take should be at least 10 seconds long. This will provide enough "room" for editing the shot later and mixing it into your video.

WIDE, MEDIUM & CLOSE SHOTS

You know what makes a video visually appealing? Variety. The wide, medium and close principle is very easy to get your head around because it's all about creating variety by recording people and objects from different distances.

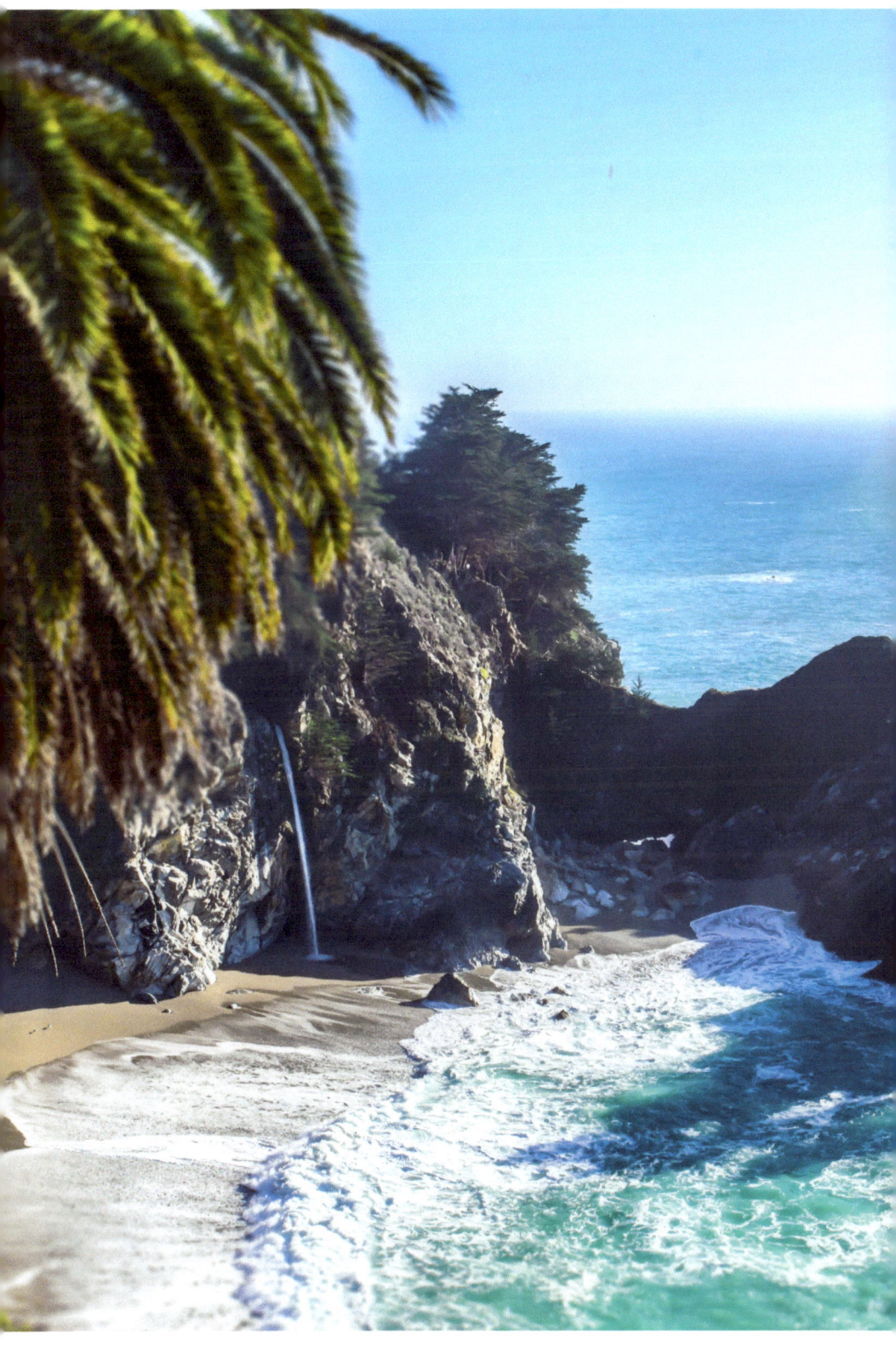

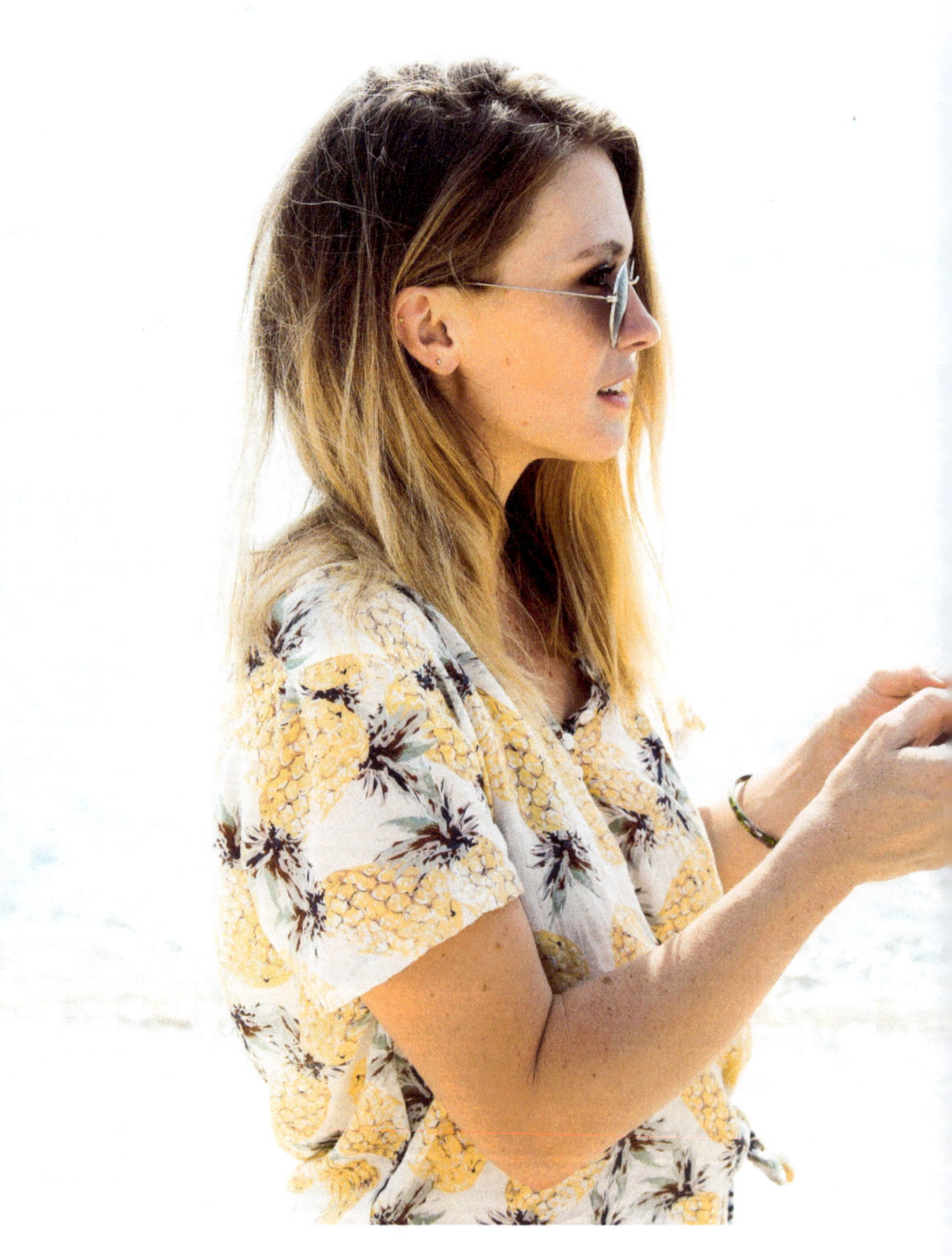

THIS COULD TRANSLATE INTO A SHOTLIST LIKE THE ONE BELOW

Shotlist

Location: Beach

Participants: Alice and Carol

Shot 1: Super wide shot from cliff overlooking beach.

Shot 2: Wide shot of subjects standing on beach.

Shot 3: Medium shot of interviewee.

Shot 4: Close up of interviewee.

If you stick to structuring your shotlist using these two principles you will have a much better time creating a visually interesting video.

CHAPTER 6

RECORDING

*"The key to sucesss is getting
a lot of small things right"*

Just as there are principles in the planning phase of your video that will significantly improve the quality of your video, following a few rules of thumb during the recording process will have you reach a much better end result.

LET'S DIVE INTO SOME USEFUL TIPS ON THE FOLLOWING

1. Basic settings and smartphone handling
2. Positioning on location

3. Instructing your subject

BASIC SMARTPHONE CAMERA SETTINGS

RULE-OF-THIRDS GRID

One of the first settings that will help improve the visual appeal of what you are recording is enabling the rule-of-thirds grid layout. This can be done on most smartphones, and will place an overlay on your recording screen for you to frame your shots properly.

When using the grid you should strive to place the people or objects in your shot at one of the two upper line intersections. You

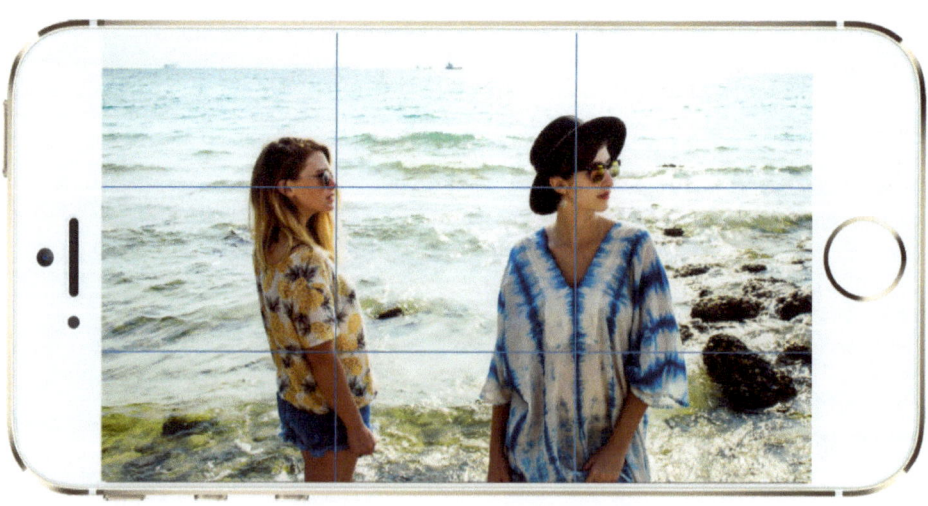

can also use the horizontal lines to make sure that your shot is levelled properly.

Using the rule-of-thirds will give your shots a lot more symmetry and naturally make them more appealing to the viewer.

EXPOSURE TOGGLE

Now this is a simple setting that can have a significant influence on the quality of your footage. Most camera apps allow you to set your exposure levels before recording by tapping the screen to choose your point of focus and then sliding your finger up and down to set the exposure.

Without going into too much detail exposure basically sets the degree of light taken in by the camera lens. Simply put, this translates into how light or dark you want your recording to be. This can be a lifesaver when the lighting conditions are less than optimal.

POSITIONING ON LOCATION

CREATING DEPTH IN YOUR FRAME

A common mistake when recording yourself or an interviewee is not thinking about the background in your shot. People often falsely assume that a neutral flat background is the best option, when in fact the opposite is true.

The function of your background should be to create depth in the frame to draw in the eyes of your viewer, so make sure to create some space behind your subject.

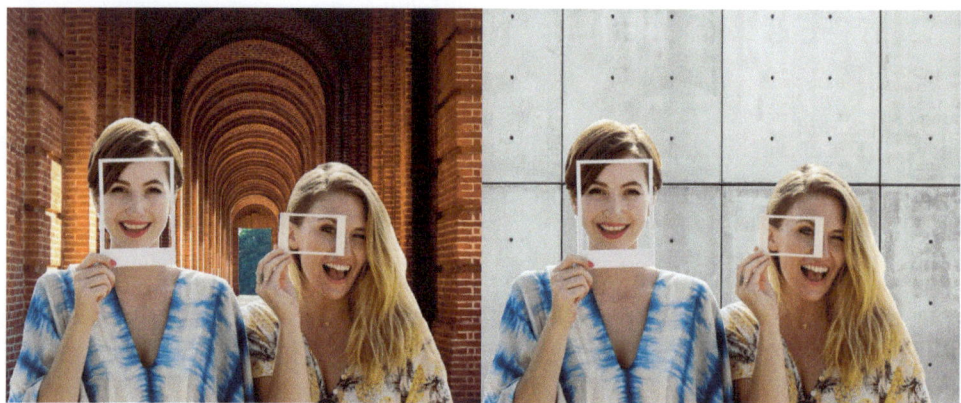

Take a look at the two examples above. Most people will find that the image on the left is more visually appealing and conveys a lot more atmosphere than the image on the right.

RECORDING AT EYE-LEVEL WHEN INTERVIEWING

A simple rule of thumb when recording yourself or other people in an interview situation is to shoot at eye-level the reason being that most of us don't look too flattering when shot from below the chin.

Likewise, shooting from above is rarely a good idea as this will make the interviewee seem small and inferior to the viewer which is not something you want to convey.

LIGHT SOURCE AWARENESS

Not being aware of the lighting at your location is a crucial mistake that can seriously detract from the quality of your footage. You should always strive to keep your lightsource behind your smartphone when recording.

The reason for keeping this in mind is that the person or object you are recording will darken and wash out if there is a stark contrast in lighting between the background at what is being filmed.

If you are shooting indoors a rule of thumb is to keep windows behind you when outside keep the sun in your back.

INSTRUCTING YOUR SUBJECT

POINT OF FOCUS

Standing in front of a camera can be quite intimidating even for people used to public speaking. There is just something about being put on the spot like that.

To loosen up the gaze of your subject a good tip is to instruct her to focus on an imaginary person right next to the lens of your smartphone.

CALMING TECHNIQUES

Once you start recording you will find that very few people are able to nail the take on the first try. Making mistakes is almost inevitable.

A smart little trick to help the person you are filming relax and get that perfect shot is to blame some of the retakes on the equipment.

Here is a suggestions on how to do just that: Let's try again Nicole i think there might have been something wrong with the audio/exposure/framing etc.

Stick to small takes at a time and don't be afraid to instruct someone in a senior position to you - remember you have a common goal, namely creating the best possible video.

Pro tip: Investing in basic gear will get you far

Although smartphone video recording has advanced tremendously the past years there are two types of additional gear you might want to invest in. The first is an external clip-on microphone which will have a huge impact on the quality of your sound. The second is a tripod, which will help keep your recordings steady and make it much easier for you to shoot consistently over a longer period of time.

CHAPTER 7

EDITING

"To receive footage that has been shot with editing in mind is a blessing."

The editing stage of a video can be a very time consuming part of the project depending on the level of detail you want to bring to the table.

At Klipworks we believe the future lies in AI-assisted editing, which is why we have built an editing engine that will do most of the work for you. You can find us in the app store - just search for Klipworks.

That being said you might want to do the editing yourself to which end we will provide you with some basic tips that will make the process easier for you.

GOOD PLANNING EQUALS GOOD FOOTAGE

Putting some thought into your planning and using your shot-list and/or storyboard properly will provide you with structure in your editing process.

It's way easier to put together a video when you have the right raw material in terms of your A- and B-roll footage.

Take note of some of our earlier suggestions on preparation and you should be in the clear.

KEEP YOUR VIDEOS SHORT

Keep your videos short. Most videos today are shared on social media which has some implications as to the ideal length of your videos.

Due to the constant bombardment of information people's attention spans are getting shorter and shorter. This is most likely why videos between 1-2 minutes are amongst the top performers on social media.

It is generally worth noting that you should be able to convey your message within a relatively short amount of time. If your videos drag out and seem to long it's most likely the result of being unclear about the message you want to convey.

DON'T OVERDO THE EDITING

One of the major pitfalls of editing is that the process quickly can turn into a vanity project keeping you going in circles on insignificant details and postponing sharing the video.

Again, simplicity is key to getting a good end result quickly. you can get far by adding your logo, some text explaining who is talking and underlying music - there are plenty of royalty free sources online.

SUMMARY

To conclude we hope you have gained some valuable knowledge during the course of reading this ebook and are inspired to get started on your video projects.

If you get one main take-away from this book let it be the realization that anyone can become a great video content producer provided they have the right knowledge to get started.

No reason for you to hang around here anymore - grab your smartphone and get started today.

FOLLOW

Follow us on social media and at klipworks.com for more stories, books and video software.

Klipworks is an innovative tech company based in Copenhagen, Denmark. The company has brought to market a groundbreaking AI-assisted video platform with the aim of empowering video content creators around the world.

KLIPWORKS

www.ingramcontent.com/pod-product-compliance
Lightning Source LLC
Chambersburg PA
CBHW040237220526

45473CB00001B/276